Our Walk With Him

one man / there for it all / to see the birth,
blossoming, and death of us all

Sofia Mae Humpheryes

BookLeaf
Publishing

India | USA | UK

Dedication

to my younger self who always wanted to write .... we're here

Preface

When I wrote this book I wrote it in isolation with no one knowing but two people I trust - this is a huge accomplishment to me and sums up my life in just a few short pages - this is my own walk with Jesus I feel many can relate to. You may not know my whole truth but I hope you know some and come to understand me and maybe yourself better. My goal is to put my truth out there rather than be popular and being authentic is extremely important to me in the process of my publishing.

Acknowledgements

to my husband who is always by my side, to god who gives me everything, to jesus who walks with light and taught me forgiveness and healing, and to the holy spirit who taught me discernment and truth - their mission was to get me here, thank you

BIRTH

I saw hundreds of faces throughout my life
and knew *nothing* about them

I saw a hundred more after that
and I thought I knew **everything**

I saw one more and realized I knew *nothing* about
humans

my quest has always been to understand
now I know I can only really know the fullness of ***myself***

Chapter 1 : BIRTH

the time of mistakes

obligations

you did not tell me with words to be a parent
but you spoke with behavior

I knew very young I was the protector and caregiver
you were the supplier, you bought the food, you gave us
beds and clothes, maybe even a few treats here and there
but you made emotional stability and affection a limited
resource
you only shared with few and those few weren't me

you passively threw affection my way while claiming my
few acceptable successes as your own

you told me everything was my fault
but who was the one protecting my sisters from your
son? who stopped the fighting? who stood up for not
only my sister's rights but yours as well?

you can claim you protected us but all I remember
during the childish fights I had with your son was you
rolling over on the couch
I remember you being submissive and weak, and letting
me take the beating instead of you
I always hoped it was worth it for you

you cling to your son and his children in a way that is
unrecognizable to me
your "I love yous" are hallow and tactical
you claim to be misunderstood and traumatized but did
you know my pain at the time? or even the person I
was?
mothers and fathers aren't perfect but you didn't even
reach for good enough
instead you grasped at scapegoating me

I think this is what you think an eldest daughter should
be

a lesson I learned in DEATH

the price of sacrament

I am quietly observing the whisperings
I am present and alive with pulse and breath and yet I
wonder ...

I wonder and ponder what my church members wonder
and ponder
I observe what my church members might be observing
and in this present moment a passing of bread and water
is passing

I think back to the blood and flesh of the Son and the
crucifix he was nailed to
would Jesus be proud of our intent during sacrament
today?
I see around me greedy hands pass everything along
everyone here is all dolled up and all dressed up head to
toe
when did church become a costume contest?
who's winning the pageant tonight?
who will be the prom queen of this sunday church
service?
you bow your meekly head with your eyes so humbly
closed
do you actually see the light of God through this prayer

or do you think whether you left the stove on at home?
as the bread touches your tongue, do you taste your
weekly sin dissolve away with your stomach juice or do
you wonder, where did they get this yummy bread?
as the holy water touches your lips do you feel sin leave
your spirit or do you ponder how off this water is
because of how cheap it is?
your mind seems distracted and your spirit seems
soulless
when the church chatter continues and the sacrament
closes I see more clearly

the water and bread seems to have a cost now
it comes with a trade for our life over one

it seems we savor the blood of Christ but we spill each
other's freely
we partake of the body of Christ but we can't be trusted
to control our own
I don't think Christ taught that He was better than our
fellowman

I think upon the vitamins I just stored and think how
this supplements me rather than others

conversion is for all you say? I'm curious whether
everyone else knows that part of the contract

I struggle with this idea of the church and become lost
often

but I found in the end the people of the church are not
defining enough
and Christ is unlike these people

what kind of Christian am I among these?
I am torn between being a member filling sits or a
Christlike follower

their criticism confuses me; they tell me not to judge, yet
what is criticism if not a form of judgment?

the absurdity of what questions are deemed acceptable is
astonishing
it shows the reality of where their discomfort truly lies

the consequence of ease

it's sad because society just picked the easier way out
when it came to our society

they wanted quick and powerful societies so they picked
                              an unfair system

rather than a patient and fair society for all
I guess, in theory, would take longer but at least it'd be
healthier and worth it, right?
  how much advancement is worth it for us to just die by
                  our own hands in a few short years?

we could live longer and better,
but all the past wanted was to be richer instead

that pattern continues today, no matter how leftist the
average man is

  betterment is a concept nowadays rather than a state of
                  being. An imaginary concept too.

our vision is too clouded
                              division is too grand
  we are too lost now due to the sins of our past societies

we will never see these concepts come to play

enjoy the life you have while you can. it's truly our last
one.

my sapphic curse [LOVERS]

the sapphic curse
the one disease they warn you about
the one they tell you to fear, the one they tell you to
ignore
there is no cure, no fixing, just suffering through it
but when I looked at her I didn't feel suffering or burden
but instead light and free
they told me you'll never be happy this way but why do I
feel just as happy then?
her skin was so pale, lovely, and silky, how can I ignore
that?
I desire her body up against me, I desire her hold, and I
desire her to be mine
those luscious lips speak to me in a way I can't ignore
every feature she hates about herself is what I love most
about her
how can I just ignore all of this?
won't that lead me to suffering?

a love that never was in DEATH

LOVERS that hurt

I knew from a very young age that my body was never
my own
I knew from a very young age the word "no" must be
softened when spoken
I learned that I must be soft to be believed
to get a point across I must be calm and collected
that anger is never justifiable
and that hysteria is a womanly disease that I must hope
to never get too much of
I learned I can't be too much or take up too much space
I also learned that I should always make space for men in
the room
three lovers of mine are burned into my memory and
body, infecting my brain and skin
the first was when I was younger, too young, and he
taught me that I am nothing but a transaction and that
my value isn't inherent but earned
my second taught me I am annoying and hard to love
and taught me I deserve pain for my wrongdoings
the last taught me that neglect is also a meaningful tool
of control and just affirmed that loving me was hard
these lovers taught me that love is limited and that love
is controlling and my fear of love is valid
yet I still craved love and still loved others regardless

I guess that's just who I am

    loves that changed me in DEATH

a body that taught me everything

aimlessly wandering the creases in my mind
through the darkness and the cloudiness
trying to make sense of the haunting touch
this bed no longer feels comfy
this body no longer feels present
these moments feels timeless in a frozen and debilitating
way
this body was my home, my only safety
rotting in my bed every night since that night
I'm becoming "that kind of victim"
the kind everyone is warned about
the angry girl
the crying girl
the statistic among so many
the helpless girl who can't be saved
I'm breaking into pieces I can't fix
I come home to a torn up bed with a sickness that can't
be cured
yet I'm demanded to go to work and act like normal with
perfect customer satisfaction scores

I used to be the light of the room but now I'm the gossip
like they know my truth

they blame this and that person and sometimes me but
they don't know who's really to blame and who's really
responsible
they wonder why I am like this
"Why is your pain so visible?"
I answer, "why isn't it more visible to you? can't you see
it?"
I am now associated with the assaulter whenever his
name is uttered or he's spoken to
judgements about me are made without knowing me or
the situation
I wish to be invisible and forgotten

would it make everyone feel better to just say I am
better?
I don't want fake guilt absolved
I don't want minds at rest in a restless situation
I fear my empowerment would feed your ego
I fear that my flourishing will be your confidence boost
I want to be sick forever for that reason
so you feel remorse with every move you make

a cure is found in BLOSSOMING

BLOSSOMING

like spring and summer, the blossoming phase of our life
brings fruitfulness and peace

color is everywhere all at once

people gather and celebrate
this season of our lives brings community, love, and hope

it can also lead to a misunderstanding that it'll never end
you forget the harsh cold winter season
while relishing the present moment of the summer's
embrace
what follows after these seasons is stored in the back of
your mind
and what stands before you is all you can see, think, and
hear

only love fills your heart
your aura glows brightly and embraces the ones you love
fully

Chapter 2 : BLOSSOMING

the season of brightness

a LOVER who crossed oceans

from so far we met
yet our souls recognized one another
soon our worlds stop
as we move towards one another
I watch our souls touch hands
they sing as their mate has finally been found

"so long," they cry out
so long have we ached for one another without knowing
each other
not knowing we needed this
two beings as one
how we could've lived without knowing our
magnificence, our impact on each other
oh a tragedy it would be
to not know love like this

you make my soul weep with joy
you wipe the tears away with worry
I exclaim my joy to you
you exclaim your love
I shiver in fear
love is painful

meaningful
beautiful
forgiving
heartbreaking
everything I fear
I fear love

you slowly become apart of my universe
this love feels like falling off a cliff
the splash from the fall is so inevitable
no one can rescue you from the splash, all you can do is
hope there's water underneath
I fall and the embrace of the water, for once, is warm and
kind
I could stay here all day but I can't drown.
I can't drown in this love
"not again," I tell myself
but you pull me in nonetheless
I start to drown, love filling my lungs
makes my heart burst
it's suffocating at first, but soon I grow comfortable
I never want to break apart from you
what have I become again? sickened with love
I feel passion once more
I have been going through the motions like a carousel
doing it's job at a park
I feel alive once more

all because of you
all of this I'm willing to feel just for you

my eternal lover in DEATH

creation

out of spontaneous energy popped the first ever being

a perfect and gracious bright light

a bodiless mass and a force to be reckoned with

it blazed with heat and beauty

not the kind of heat that can burn you but the kind that snuggles us close

this matter was one we cannot possibly conceive of with our imagination or sight

it was the ultimate being, the one, the perfection, the model of all that is good

He was made and was never ending
He existed in a void of power, in a womb of dimensions
He moved through everything, both swiftly and slowly, all at once

in this space was the unorganized state of the universe, he touched every corner he could

He observed just this:

Nebulas and suns and stars, dimensions and spaces of
nothingness

He did nothing but this:

With a bright blow of energy from His newly made
power He swiped and created sense to the mess

suddenly, it became a universe, everything became one

this raw energy formed the earth, the sun, the stars,
everything we know which we can see and feel

the mysterious yet felt being had just only just began
something that we will soon come to know

the body that taught me forgiveness

sadness and trauma are both deep things that need to be experienced, witnessed, and solved by our inner selves

when we have the help of others it can be an amazing aid
community helps us grow confidence in our healing journey

I hope to pass on the wisdom to you that healing is possible, transformation is beautiful and fulfilling

redemption is not only something achievable but inherent to us merely because we are flawed humans

the road to redemption can be long but not impossible

there will be a day when you feel you are forgiven and a day where you have forgiven yourself

I forgive you, move on now without guilt

the lament we sing

the lament we sing
a tune dark and dreary
cords being plucked at, flutes wheezing, and a loud
wailing can be heard

our generation is wailing along
we sing with the dead
which haunts and plagues societies
a sort of mourning consumes us and we carry it on our
backs
a manifestation of our shared suffering

a concept of us exists but no one hears our truth
you dress us up in your corporate outfits but you never
see the burnt skin under the fabric
you light us on fire and pour gasoline on us to put it out
we learned to stop, drop, and roll but not how to find
water to keep it out
you point and laugh at us but never point at yourself or
fellow men, the real jesters

we all are lost by force and forgotten as a consequence
the lament we sing is one passed down to us
it is never forgotten between generations

you can try to make us forget but we know the melody
very well
we sing of our perseverance with a tune of melancholy

our strength comes from the heavy trials
yes we have built up muscle but is that fair?
the lament we sing will always play until it's heard by
the right people and handled in the right way

faith is blind

faith is holding power in your heart, a little feeling of inspiration that causes you to cover your eyes. you move forward with trust that something is guiding you home. you may stumble, maybe even fall, and the ground feels shaky and uneven, you may feel afraid and lost, but you're positive everything will be okay and you'll be home in a warm embrace. the city is wild, and noises are everywhere, and you realize that the city is way more complicated than ever before. but you know, not through logic, not through reason, but faith. the warmth in your heart fills your body. it's blind yet very real.

you arrive home, in one piece and whole, born again, refreshed and renewed. you know you are home, cuddled in your favorite blanket, in a warm embrace of invisible hands. you know you are understood and loved. you acknowledge the journey here, but you do not dwell on it. for the life you live is peaceful henceforth, and all due to your endurance among the stumbly paths. you wait for others to find their faith, and that they come home to your embrace as well as His. you acknowledge not all will find their way but you pray their paths are fulfilling nonetheless. you wish serenity among all and that all demons are fought with might and chivalry.

you thank those invisible hands and sleep with peace
and virtue - prayers being said and manifested through
the dreams that follow.

the three key beliefs

25

Jesus taught me to walk like him, to hold in my heart
three key beliefs

to hold justice, forgiveness and love in my heart at all
times

for justice keeps things fair, forgiveness keeps things
kind, and love keeps everything, every intention, pure

DEATH

winter is here
it's dark and clear
that everything here is meant to be here

the past summer is a foggy memory
the cold chills a burn on your skin
you want everything that's not this

why can't things be the way they were?
because it was never meant to be that way forever
you must rest and reset
organize and prioritize
what is valuable? what is salvageable? what is worth it
anymore?
it's so hard to know through all these snow storms
the isolation alone will drive you insane
the reward is so far out of sight but never unreachable

Chapter 3 : DEATH

it is now time to weigh the value

a lesson about families

my caretaker walked the field of our house with selective
care
picking and choosing which plants she loved more
nourishing and loving each one differently
I was a weed among plants and as such must be yanked
at
if I'm not I will infect the garden and be a threat to the
flourishment of the field
so they yanked at me - ripping out each roots and stem
and yet I grew back each time to be
only to be yanked at again
every year I grew more and more
more weeds and roots to be yanked at
what I learned about the field is no one is safe
the rose wasn't even safe amongst the weeds and it
wasn't the weeds fault that they weren't safe
the caretaker was in control this whole time
roses were happy to believe that I was the source
but each year their petals were snipped for a milky bath
and each time I wasn't the one holding the shears
some family units run like fields
they sacrifice a lamb to save the farm
I found there are families who will love my
overabundant growth

they will let my roots run wild in the earth below
my roots do not imply ruin to the field but implies the
loss of control which the caretaker cannot tame

the lesson : ***we have a right to freedom and autonomy***

a lesson in shame

amongst the world of man lives a land of secrecy
where harlots run about
the world whispers about this land with harsh tones
the world will side glance those who come from the land
it's visible on the land's skin that they are different from
the world
they remind the Earth of the flesh they live in
the skin that craves gratification
expression is a mirror to gaze upon worldly sins
Jesus knows the land well
all it's hills and trails are wandered frequently
He helps cultivate the land without preconception
the world knows this but they fail to understand this
He asks us all to understand radically
He demands we till the land of our flesh with respect
He asks we nourish other lands with love
He challenges us to hold space and time for others
without the desire for control

the lesson : *shame is a means of control that should not tie us down*

a lesson in loving others

when you feel a drought in your soul
a famine through your bones
a hollowness in your pores
when you realize everything is empty and barren
you rethink on those that till your land
those who you thought were responsible
you realize you're the best keeper of your land
as you water your crops very sweetly and protectively
the snowy landscape becomes a field of fresh berries and
flowers that sweet bees suckle from
feeding a village with a bare field has left bellies needing
more
a farm can feed a village but the village must also feed
the farmer

the lesson : *we must all care for each other*

eternal companions

the passion of two lovers
bodies as new as their first day
a promise untarnished by time
every night hand in hand under the moonlight
they believed this was forever

though as time went on they grew further and further
apart journeying on
they spent their days with new things
the thought of the immortal lover would cross their mind
yet the thought was never enough to feel that ache for
each other
they loved others
they felt the rush of life separate from each other
then the moonlight fell upon them again
the memory of touch flooded in
the ache came back
they began wondering how the other was
they traced the lines on their palms to mimic the touch
of each other
it was never the same
they realized all that they've experienced was without
their other half
their smiles, their laughter, their joy had a hint of

sadness for a while
as time passed they only felt grief and sorrow
they by instinct knew they had to find one another

they met with the fear of perception
yet when eyes gazed upon each other that fear flew into
the wind
they danced into each other's arms
the lovers spoke, "my soul continued craving you"
hand in hand under the moonlight
the soul remembers, as they learned
when the world burned down, they became burnt into
the ground within the ashes of the fire, forever
embracing and yet still alive

not even time nor death could untie the knot of love

thoughts on GOD

I think we need to remember that church is not just a
place for the "healed" or "the followers of said religion"
but instead a hospital or rehab for the sinners of the
world

while not everyone will find their truth in this lifetime I
think many will be genuinely changed in the hereafter

to judge a path and compare it to yours, to measure their
life to your expectations is a failure on our part and not
theirs

I think people will be surprised in the hereafter who is
forgiven and who is not.

I see everyone is exhausted by the expectations of
change
by the markers we require everyone to be at
really no one changes on anyone's time but God's and
their own

if we face shame from ourselves on "I should be here" or
"I should be there"
or we force that upon someone else

just know that yes, God's timing is perfect but so isn't
yours

trust your intuition
trust your heart
trust in the universe
all timing is perfect and if we slip back, we can always
climb back up.

and for the judges of the world and people whom aren't
God please put yourself to your own expectations
I truly believe you know you won't ever measure up to
them
which shines a light to the source of their motive
no person is perfect
which is logic we should all hold for others and not just
ourselves.

to the hurt and forgotten I hear your sadness and see
your struggle
I see and feel it for I am willing to admit I too am weak,
sad, and struggling
this note is for you to know we all are in someway
perfection does not exist
we all fail at something
some aren't good at sports or video games
some fail at understanding the heart and the soul

I love all my fellow men
the flawed and the supposed perfect - I nurse the broken
and live with the sorted out.

the lesson *: we are not perfect and never will be,
including me, only God himself can judge someone's
progress*

the immortal man

one immortal man
a man left to rot on earth with no decay evident
mind and soul aged and perserved
with a body as clean and pristine as a young man of 20

when societies crumble
when castles and towers fall and nations burn and
tumble
He was there amongst the ashes and bones
He was living and breathing while the young and old lie
in the same grave
not even the sun exploding and the earth burning could
char Him

in space He floats amongst the pieces of earth until stars
burn out and darkness is all that's left
He was there for it all
the birth and blossoming of people
people held the curiosity to know more
He realized death doesn't pick favorites, for it happens to
all but Him
the one man stands before it all, with one question for
them all, "who here knows it all?"
the crowds fall silent

He has seen it all from beginning to end

while He sits beneath the burning sun, on a chair made
of red wood, and the sky falls upon Him, He realizes He
knew it all
for the wise don't know
for the kind don't know
for the ignorant don't know
the young and old don't know
He found humans have to see it all, and one life is not
enough to know it all
but He sees and He knows
for what is God if not a man who sees it all? The past,
the present, the future and the individual
knowledge is built on knowing, and knowing is built
through experience and the heart feels what it knows
and the mind believes what it knows
the man sits quietly even when He's surrounded by
darkness
He knows no sound can be heard, but it wouldn't matter
if it could
this is like His death, a time to rest, the awareness that
this is peace and the answers have been answered
a coffin may not be His bed during this nor is the Earth
embracing His body
and yet He is comforted by the pressure of space and the
darkness which feels like sleep

a blanket may not be around Him but the memory of
warmth and love keeps Him warm
humanity is beautiful, He said, in all it's galore
amen, He speaks onto His spirit

Our walk with Him never ends
But right here is where we must separate
Until we meet again, a solemn promise that we'll find
him along our path
We say this in the name of Jesus Christ, amen

www.ingramcontent.com/pod-product-compliance
Lightning Source LLC
La Vergne TN
LVHW021312200726
843509LV00012B/1881